Mothering

MOTHERING

POETRY & PROSE

RHIANNON HENDERSON

ISBN: 9780992397234

For the newborn mums, the toddler mums, the child mums, the teen mums, the adult mums, the exhausted mums, and the lonely mums...

But especially for the solo mums.

May you remember how truly incredible you are.

And, for my daughter Beatrix.
May this serve as my forever unfinished
love letter to you.

Contents

Acknowledgements

Ah, there's an argument to be said for acknowledgements, whether we should add them to our works or not.

It's a personal choice, but especially in the case of *Mothering*, I would be extremely remiss to skip such a perfect opportunity to thank and acknowledge those who have helped me not only with this book, but with my motherhood journey thus far.

First and foremost, my daughter Beatrix. Bunny girl, thank you for making me a mother. This entire book is for you. I may never finish printing photos for your baby books, but I hope this will make up for it.

To My Mum and Dad. Thank you for always supporting me, especially when I decided to have a baby solo, for loving my daughter the way you do, and for being the best Grandma and Grumpy Bunny could ask for.

Kristine, thank you for being one of my oldest friends, and always supporting me in absolutely everything I do. You are the definition of ride or die. I know that you always have my back when I really need it. I have loved watching you become a mother to Frankie and can't wait to watch you both grow.

Monica, thank you for being the friend I didn't even know I needed. You have raised two beautiful little girls who are the best role models for Bunny, and I love watching their little girl gang blossom too. Your support and friendship mean so much to me, and I appreciate you more than you know.

Lauren, thank you for your help and advice in editing this book, for your unwavering support and understanding of all of my endeavours, and for showing me from the day we met, what a great mother looks like. You showed me that motherhood could be an incredible adventure, and I am forever thankful.

Samantha Gunn, for the hundredth time I ask, is it still a postpartum doula if your child is no longer a baby? Thank you for helping me find my footing in motherhood, for supporting me from day one, feeding me, encouraging me, and for your support and friendship for all this time.

Nanny Jess, thank you for being a constant safe place for my daughter for almost two years. Having someone love her as much as you do, made my life so much easier. You helped me become the mother I am today, and you will always be a part of our family.

To the one who has held space for me and allowed me to live my life authentically, to chase my dreams, to become a mother, and to grow in ways I never knew I could, thank you.

Finally, thank you to all my pocket friends. Instagram and the friendships I have made on there, helped me through the isolation of parenting for the first time in a pandemic. The support and friendship I have found from so many of you, some new friends and some old but renewed, has encouraged me to be authentically myself, without fear of judgement. Thank you.

That's the thing about motherhood.

It destroys you.
And it heals you.

Looking Glass

Who was I
before I was
a mother?

Where is she
the woman that
came before?

I find remnants
now and then,
fragments from the past.

Like relics
of another time,
through the looking glass.

Unexpected

You burst into my world
and changed it.
Without warning,
I looked into your eyes
and realised
I was looking at my heart
beating
outside of my body.
From that day forward
I knew,
the love I have for you
will forever be
all consuming.

Wait, what?

Is it just me,
or is it mind blowing
to anyone else
that they just
let you have a baby?

You made it,
sure.
But then...
You just take it home.
Into your world.
A world that feels
so drastically different,
yet is exactly the same.

Nothing has changed,
but you are not the same.

3am

White noise,
heavy eyes,
tiny lungs,
so very loud.

Soft skin,
wet shirt,
quiet gulps,
such little nails.

Warm breath,
soft sighs,
fluttering eyelids,
no one else around.

Mother Knows Best

Drowsy but awake,
don't feed to sleep,
always in a cot,
never in the bed.

Breast is always best,
but if not, at least they're fed.
"Here's a list of rules for you"
is what the midwife said.

There are no rules to motherhood,
this I've learnt for sure,
for as much as you can hope to do.
another will do more.

Packet food or
homemade blends,
bottle or the breast,
there's one thing
I can guarantee,

As a mother,
you know best.

I don't remember who I was
before I met you.
I can't quite figure out,
where that woman went.
Like a switch,
it just happened,
The old me was gone,
a new one in her place.
That woman I knew so well,
just an echo.
A soft shadow in the background,
always slightly out of focus.

You weren't the only one
born on that day.

I was too.

Atmospheric

It's you and me, kid.
Just the two of us.
Our little bubble
a tiny world,
a whole universe.
In the air surrounding us,
magic,
and love,
and joy
mix with the oxygen.
Our own atmosphere
and there's nowhere else
I'd rather be.

Oceans

My love for you
my darling child,
so strong,
so wide,
so deep.

Expansive
just like
The sea,
its waves
crashing over me.

Becoming

I write so much
about the changes.
Becoming a mother,
becoming *your* mother
changed me.
Intrinsically,
Inherently,
So undeniably.
And yet
at the same time
I have never felt more like me.
Becoming your mother
allowed me to become
the most authentic version
of myself.

Matrescence

The journey to becoming
everything
I was always meant to be.

The exploration of myself
and you,
and us together.

The strength in existing
in this time and place
of growth and pain

The emergence of my favourite self.
The reimagining of life
and how I thought it would be.

I thought
that I was ready.
I did everything
on the list.

I washed your little onesies.
I can't explain
how they were
so small,
yet so big
at the same time.

I wasn't ready,
for all the things
that weren't
on the list.

Like how you go to sleep,
and when you wake
you've grown again,
overnight.

And for the day
I packed away those
same onesies
now just small,
too small
for you.

Motherhood

A newfound strength
grows within me,
I am capable
of more than I imagined

That newborn bubble is intense,
but I promise
you'll make it through.

I have never been more challenged,
still, I know we'll make it through.
We make an epic team my love,
together, me and you.

This Time Around

How can you miss someone you've
never met?
I just did.
I knew your soul
long before
your time on this earth
this time around.

Untold Strength

It's interesting
that women
are rarely told
of the strength
in motherhood.

Imagine
if we knew,
unequivocally,
that we held
a warrior
within us.

I wonder
if we'd see
the power
behind our eyes
as we looked
at our reflection?

If only
we were told
the truth,
then maybe
we'd see ourselves
differently.

The Flamboyant Return

Motherhood is so intense
for the flamingo
that she loses
her colour.

The vibrant
and bold shade
that makes her
so famous,
fades.

But
it returns,
day by day,
when that phase
slowly ends.

When she can
focus on herself,
nourish herself,
heal herself,
it returns.

Her vivid colour,
her striking hue.
It's just a matter of time
til she is brighter
and better than ever

So, when you feel
depleted,
faded,
drained
of all your colour.

Remember
this isn't forever.
This is just
a season.
This season of motherhood.

I promise,
your sparkle,
your vibrance,
your dazzling radiance
will return.

Cosmic Calls

I often tell the story
when asked about my plans,
of why I had a baby solo
without a "lovely man".

Well.

Without going through the obvious,
all the reasons that I could,
I always tell the truth.

I just knew that you were waiting for
me.
I felt your soul call mine.
I used to dream about you.
I woke up one morning and knew
I had to make you a body.
And while that sounds so insane,
I've never felt anything more
overwhelmingly
than the pull to create you.

All throughout my pregnancy
I never once felt alone.
I always knew that I was doing
exactly what I was meant to do.

So, I want you to know,
back then
when you were born,
and even now…
It's always been you.

All The Things They Never Said

"The days are long"
They said.

"The years are short"
They said.

But I didn't understand.

The days and nights
merged into one,
the never-ending stretch
of broken nights,
of tiny cries,
of scratchy eyes.

You fall asleep next to a newborn,
and wake up next to an infant.
The change is subtle
yet indisputable.
Such is the
paradox of time.

All The Things They Never Said
Part Two

They never told me,
or maybe I just
never truly understood.
The exquisite torture,
the beautiful agony,
of watching your baby
change.

The Hourglass

Minutes turned into hours.
Before long, those hours turned into
days.
Days merged into nights,
nights faded into mornings,
mornings turned into afternoons.

Before I realised
those minutes
and hours
and days
had turned
into weeks
and months
and years.

The Magic Of You

I swear you grow
little by little,
before my very eyes.
Your limbs lengthening,
eyes shining,
hair sprouting,
as I look on in wonder,
honoured to witness
the magic of you.

Kintsugi

When pottery is broken
in the Japanese culture,
it is rebuilt,
lovingly.
The cracks and imperfections
highlighted with beauty,
a flash of gold, silver, or platinum
drawing attention
to the changes,
or breakage
it has sustained.

I've never heard
of something quite so perfect
to describe the beautiful
and agonising
process of matrescence

Cracked,
weakened,
splintered,
but not abandoned.
Loved,
repaired,

made whole again.
The glint of gold

a beautiful reminder
that who you are
is both a mix
of who you used to be,
and who you will be.

The woman you were before
does not exist in the same way,
but she does still exist.
Your heart was just cracked open,
healed and put back together
bigger
and better.
To be filled to the brim
with more love
than you could have
ever imagined.

Ill-prepared

Preparation…
If only it were that simple.
Nothing can prepare
for the ultimate shift
from self centred living
to selfless sacrifice.
Mind, body, spirit
devoted to another.
A tiny little soul
who chose you
to be its mother.

Can you believe
that there's such a thing
as "mothers' wrist"?

An injury
named after
the ultimate athlete,
the mother.

As if
we didn't know
that parenting
was an extreme sport.

Fundamental Changes

Even science says
almost all female mammals
go through these
fundamental changes
during the process
of becoming a mother

Both pregnancy and birth
alter the hormones,
the structure,
the size of the neurons,
the brain chemistry,
the changes are
not just the physical body.

So, when they talk
about leaving behind
all that came before,
and becoming someone new,
someone different,
The Mother.

Know that it's not something
so easily controlled.
That trying harder
won't make it easier.
Because even science says
you're going through
fundamental changes.

The Landscape Doesn't Look The Same

We often hear the term "It takes a village", when discussing having a baby, and raising children.

What is usually omitted, is that we don't always have one.

Becoming a mother has so many amazing parts, experiences that make your heart swell, and small quiet moments that fill your cup in ways you didn't realise you needed.

But there are also really hard moments, really difficult experiences, and overwhelmingly sad parts to the path of motherhood.

One that is so little talked about, is how lonely it can be. Not just late at night when the world is asleep, but day to day.

The friends you thought would be in
your life forever... sometimes‚ they
don't make the journey with you.

The sadness surrounding the loss of
those friendships can be overwhelming.

When we begin to prioritise our
children, the tiny humans who rely on
us to survive, other relationships are
often the casualties.

The friend who you thought would
always be there, the one whose tiny
babies you held, with all the kid's
birthday parties you attended, maybe
one day they won't be that person for
you.

Maybe they won't support you through
your first few months of motherhood
the way you supported them. Perhaps
they won't even give your child a first
birthday card or gift, or even
acknowledge the day at all.

And maybe you never notice the small
ways in which they don't show up for
you, until you look back and realise,
they never really did at all.

Motherhood can be lonely, and we can
lose so much of our old life, friends
turn to strangers, and the world we
lived in before just doesn't look the
same anymore.

There is light though, and new
friendships to be made. We are broken
down in the process of becoming, and
your own baptism of fire will show you
who your true friends are.

Sometimes we think we are left with
nobody, the life detox that is childbirth
can definitely shatter all expectations
and disprove all of those "I can't wait
to meet the baby" messages.

Slowly but surely, you'll build your new
village, a friend from mothers' group,
an old acquaintance, another mum you

meet at the park, a handful of pocket friends from social media, or even your next door neighbour. Just as you didn't notice the friendships you had were fading away, before you know it, you'll realise you've built your own little village. The landscape won't look the way you expected, but it will be breathtaking.

So, motherhood is lonely, and you will lose a lot along the way… but I promise you, what you gain will be far more than what you left behind.

No Regrets

Wrapped up tightly
in your little plastic box.
Sleeping soundly
a little smile flits across
your sweet face
and my heart swells.

No regrets
I think to myself.

Maybe just one
A small voice whispers
from somewhere within.

You are so perfect
so beautiful
so incredible
so surreal.

I have never before
wanted to share you
nor experience this life
with anyone else.

But seeing you here...
For just a moment
I wish you had another.
Another set of eyes to gaze upon your
beauty.
Another heart to be consumed by love
for you.
Another world to be shattered by your
birth.

In a blink
that thought is gone
when I remember
that I never have to share you.
These moments are just ours.
I get to love you
like nobody else can.

No regrets.
I think again
with a smile
as a tear creeps
down my cheek.

That tiny voice
from somewhere within
echoes.

No regrets.
Not even one.

How can I explain
the beautiful torture,
the painful honour,
the exquisite torment,
the heart-breaking privilege
the overwhelming pride and
devastation
of being a mother?

All of the reading,
the books and the blogs,
nothing could have prepared me
for this journey.
The tiny hand in mine
growing marginally
every day.

Nobody ever told me,
the milestones are so bittersweet.
Or maybe they did,
and I didn't understand.
It's a special kind of heartbreak
to watch your baby
grow into your child.

The First Year

The first year of motherhood has been
so incredible.
As I look back at photos and videos,
remembering the struggles,
it's mind-blowing how far away it all
seems. How inconsequential in the
scheme of
her life thus far.
They say it gets better, easier.
That when you're in the thick of it,
you can't see the light… and it's true.
Next thing you know, you're looking
back at a year's worth of memories,
some hazy from lack of sleep,
but a million shimmering moments that
flit in and out of your mind just the
same.
I write this at 1am with a half-asleep
almost one-year-old on my chest,
who has flipped back and forth across
the bed for the last hour.
Teasing me with a few moments of still
silence before flopping back like a fish

out of water, crawling back over to
plant her head on my chest.
I wouldn't change this.
Her little breath on my face,
her hand tangled in my hair,
her heartbeat so close to mine.
It's everything I didn't even realise
I was dreaming of.
When I thought of my life with my
daughter,
I thought of adventures.
Experiencing the corners of the world
with her.
And yet, the biggest adventure has been
getting to know this tiny person I
made, and the person I've become
along the way. Experiencing our own
little world in ways that I never even
thought of.
Countless hours of sleepy cuddles,
breathing in her scent,
sitting in the quiet stillness.
A billion tiny fragments of time that
will be gone before I know it.

I look across at her body now splayed
across the bed next to me and realise
her size.
She's so much bigger than I
remember.
I could have sworn she fit snugly in the
crook of my arm yesterday,
and now, when she's snuggled in,
her feet extend past my knees.
Where did the last year go?
It feels simultaneously like an entire
lifetime has passed me by,
and yet also that I blinked for a
moment too long on one of those first
few days with a newborn and woke up
with a one-year-old.
I thought I'd be a good mum, at least,
that I wouldn't do a terrible job.
I suppose nobody ever chooses to go
into motherhood, thinking they'll do a
bad job.
I don't think I really considered who I
would become on the other side of her
existence.
I've surprised myself, actually.
In a good way, I think.

I love who I am.
I love being a mother...
More specifically,
I love being *her* mother.

Every day, I wake up to her smiling
face
and I can't believe how lucky I am
to spend the rest of my life hanging out
with and getting to know my
magnificent daughter.
What a totally mind-blowing, core-
shaking and truly remarkable year that
first year of motherhood has been.
Well, only a lifetime to go.

The Unspoken Fear

How lucky am I to have such a
beautiful soul to share this lifetime
with?
I was terrified of motherhood.
I watched friends struggle with
parenting, telling me how much my life
would change and how hard it is.
While it has its challenges, I am so glad
those experiences I watched are not my
own.
Yes, we struggled with sleep - sort of.
Sure, I never showered alone.
And I don't get time to myself when
the baby sleeps.
And the only alone time I get is when
she is cared for so that I can run
errands, and businesses, maintain
friendships,
book doctors' appointments and exist
as my own person.
I've never really had someone come
shopping with me or sit in the car so I
could grab some groceries.

I've never been able to run out for a
coffee,
or a manicure or have a night off to
catch up on some sleep.
But that's how I like it.
I love hanging out with my tiny
human.
Her laugh makes my whole body
sparkle. You know what I mean, don't
you?
My world is magical and
shimmery because she's in it, and I am
so thankful she's picked me to be her
mum.

The Small Moments

I watch the sky
changing colours,
close my eyes
pull up the covers,
snuggle down close
my nose in your hair.
I love this the most,
these moments we share.

In The Blink Of An Eye

One day
you're holding a tiny baby.
You're bleeding,
and sore,
and tired
like you've never been before.
But you're happy,
in a way you can't explain.
Intrinsically,
unexplainably
joyful.

You blink
your eyes close for just
a moment or two
and then
she's giggling,
with a tooth you'd not noticed before.
But you're sad
in a way you can't explain
Intrinsically,
unexplainably
sorrowful.

And that
in the simplest terms
is motherhood.

Rhiannon Henderson

I wasn't ready
For you to grow up so soon.

I wasn't ready.

"Mummy!"
Your tiny voice calls out
a sweet siren song
calling me to your side.

Rhiannon Henderson

It happened in a way I can't explain
like a bushfire.
Tiny sparks just smouldering,
I looked away for a second
and it was out of my control.
You were growing up.

Broken Promises

I promised myself
I'd never forget
the way you felt
curled in my arms
the first few days.
You were so small,
almost weightless
but so heavy with love.

I've broken that promise
one thousand times over.
Each time I vow
not to break it again.
Now your long lanky limbs
spill over my arms
when I cradle you close
and the love that I feel
spills out of my heart.
Overflowing
like the tears in my eyes.
The promise
is broken again
and the memories
have already begun to fade.

It Was Only You

I never want you to feel
like you were not enough.
That maybe you were seen to be
a consolation prize,
a fraction of the perfect life,
the dream of a suburban wife.
But that was never
what I hoped for,
not the dream I had for me.

You have always been
and will always be,
the one and only thing
I ever truly wanted.

The Mornings

There will be mornings
I'll wake up alone,
without a knee in my side
or a foot in my back.

And there will be nights
when I'll sleep all the way through,
stretched out like a starfish,
no other head on my pillow.

I'll drink a hot cuppa,
eat a full piece of toast,
even the crusts,
I'm sure I'll love those the most.

I'll take a hot shower
without anyone else,
and I won't trip on your bath toys,
or use baby wash on myself.

I'll take time to get ready,
getting dressed on my own.
My lipsticks are all safe,
No cartoons on my phone.

I'll walk out the door,
I won't be counting to three.
I'll not have checked in the mirror
for any stickers on me.

But I'll still see you there,
your ruffled hair on my pillow,
sprawled across the doona
when I open my eyes.

I'll still hear your questions
and all of your songs,
like your shower time tunes
and the ones you made up.

I'll still feel the tug
of your hand on my skirt,
the ghost of the years past
always in my heart.

One day you'll be grown
and things won't be the same,
but I'll relive
the small memories of you
for all of my days.

Welcome To The Club

The tiny baby
cradled in my arms
wiggles
and scrunches her nose.
Her little mouth opens
and a feeble little cry escapes.
"Baby!" you say,
pointing and patting her softly.
"Mummy, the baby cry!"
you smile up at me.
Shushing the little one
I place her in your arms
ever so gently
and you hold her
with pride and excitement.

Suddenly I am struck
with the realisation
that you are no longer
a baby.

Your Aunty and I exchange a look
as we watch our children
meet for the first time.

A moment I'm not sure
either of us ever thought much of.
The day when
my 27-month-old
would be
cuddling her 27-hour old.

The two of us
part of the same club
but in totally different places.
Her curled in a hospital bed
just starting her new journey,
feeling like there's forever
before hers is this grown.
Me perched on a chair
looking back
at the road we've travelled,
remembering my tiny newborn,
wondering where the time went
and when you grew this big.

In that moment
I knew time didn't move
the same way
anymore.

I know that one morning
I'll wake so well rested.
I won't hear you snoring,
a little congested.
You'll be in your bed
asleep at sunrise.
Not sticking your fingers
in my nose and my eyes.

I drop you off at daycare
Now I'm sobbing in a store,
feeling like I've ruined it all.
I wonder when I'll work it out,
what the best thing is for us.
Am I doing the right thing
or am I screwing it all up?
Will our bond be broken?
Will you think that you're not loved?
Will you grow up to hate me?
Am I messing you all up?

To My Daughter

One day you might find yourself
wrapped up in your own
motherhood bubble.
Your own little one
cuddled close
in the darkest part
of the night.
And you might feel
like nobody else in the world
is there with you.
I promise you,
the love I have for you
will surround you then,
just as it does now.

Team No Sleep

I don't know if I'll ever sleep again,
not really.
I think I'll always wake
at the slightest noise
on high alert for your voice.
Forever listening out,
just in case.
When I heard
that motherhood changes you
deeply
on a cellular level,
I nodded,
without realising
that never being able to sleep
deeply, and properly
ever again
would be one of those changes.

Am I Enough?

I hope that I'm enough for you.
Love you enough,
say it enough,
hug you enough,
play enough,
laugh enough,
dance enough,
put my phone down enough.

Even on my worst days,
I hope that I'm enough for you.

Chapters Of You

It was over before I knew it.
The newborn crunch,
the helpless wail,
the snuffly nose,
the tiny hiccups,
the soft sighs,
the unfocused eyes.

In the blink of an eye, it became
the furniture climbs,
the excited squeal,
the drooly chin,
the messy face,
the joyful giggle,
the reaching arms.

Another blink and it was
the run through the park,
the ABC's,
the babycino dates,
the skinned knees,
the incessant questions,
the "I love you"'s.

I'm scared but thrilled to blink again,
to watch your life unfold
and see you grow older.
Because time moves differently
like our own hourglass,
and so many chapters of you
are over before I know it.

Rhiannon Henderson

My Favourite

I don't want to always be my best,
I want to be my favourite.
My favourite version of myself,
whatever that is,
whenever that is.
I want to always try my best
as each day begins,
even if that's not
the most incredible version of me,
I want it to be my favourite.
Because some of my favourite
versions of myself
are milk covered,
hair matted,
pajama clad,
morning breathed,
makeup free,
just you, and me.

We Made It

The days feel like years,
the minutes dragging by.
Sleep pulling at my consciousness
like the breeze
pulls the dandelions.

Night-time is always the hardest.
The loneliness creeps in.
Everything is harder,
louder
but quieter.

It feels like we might not make it
til the morning.
It feels like I'm the only one
in the world holding
a screaming baby.
The darkness is heavy,
making it hard to breathe.

But the sun rises
in more ways than one.
Somehow everything looks better in
the soft light of dawn.

I look back and realise
the years feel like days,
the days feel like seconds,
the darkest nights
drift away
into the brightest daylights
and we made it.

Mothering

I wish I could rewind and do it all over
again.
I guess that's motherhood.
So excited for the future but so
nostalgic for the past.
I can remember so many tiny moments
and they make my heart sing.
I might not remember the exact first
time you laughed.
But I can hear a million little chuckles
when I think of you.
I might not know the exact time I
changed from "mama" to "mummy."
But I can hear your little voice clearly
calling out both in my mind.
I truly cannot remember the first time
you took my hand in yours.
But I can feel so many times your little
fingers gripping mine in my memory.
Being your mother has been nothing
like I anticipated, yet exactly like I
dreamed, and somehow so much
more.
It has been… everything.